First published in paperback in 2016 by Wayland

Copyright © Wayland, 2016

Editor: Nicola Edwards

Designer: Rocket Design (East Anglia) Ltd

Illustrations by Alex Paterson

Dewey number: 331.7'00938–dc23

ISBN: 978 0 7502 9934 3

Library eBook ISBN: 978 0 7502 8744 9

10 9 8 7 6 5 4 3 2 1

MIX
Paper from
responsible sources
FSC® C104740

Wayland, an imprint of

Hachette Children's Group

Part of Hodder and Stoughton

Carmelite House

50 Victoria Embankment

London EC4Y 0DZ

An Hachette UK Company

www.hachette.co.uk

www.hachettechildrens.co.uk

Printed and bound in China

All photographs supplied by
The Art Archive (www.art-archive.com)
except for p4 (bottom), p5 (top), p9,
p17 (bottom), Shutterstock.com

within!

The Best (& Worst) Jobs in
ANCIENT GREECE

Clive Gifford

WAYLAND

CONTENTS

THE JOB MARKET
IN ANCIENT GREECE

So you're looking for employment in ancient Greece? There are plenty of jobs to choose from!

Ancient Greece flourished from around 800 BCE after waves of settlers moved to the region bordering the Aegean Sea in southern Europe. Lasting for over a thousand years, the civilization wasn't a single nation or empire. It was made up of many different city-states, including Sparta, Corinth, Larissa and Athens, with colonies later dotted around the Mediterranean Sea, including Ephesus (in present day Turkey), Syracuse (on the island of Sicily) and Cyrene (on the coast of Egypt). So be prepared to travel by sea if you want to visit different places in the ancient Greek world.

MACEDONIA

GREECE

Delphi

Argos · Corinth

Olympia · · Mycenae · Athens

· Sparta

Aegean Sea

TURK

Mediterranean Sea

The ancient Greek world developed amongst the rocky, hilly Aegean peninsula and the large numbers of islands close by before extending out across the lands bordering the Mediterranean Sea.

Invented by the scientist Archimedes of Syracuse, the Archimedean screw helped farmers to raise water from a low-lying water source. Similar designs are still used to this day.

The ancient Greeks valued learning, maths, science, philosophy and the arts. They invented or pioneered many of the things we take for granted today, from the first-known plays and theatres to coin-operated vending machines and trial by jury in courts. Among their many inventions were the crane for lifting heavy loads, the watermill, central heating and the alarm clock! With such a brainy bunch, competition for the top jobs must have been fierce. To see what jobs were on offer in ancient Greece and which were the best and worst, read on…

Ancient Greek potters produced beautiful vases richly decorated with scenes and images of gods.

ODD JOB

OUCH!

Some sportsmen earned a living by taking part in competitions, but these could be brutal. During a bareknuckle boxing bout at the ancient Olympics, Eurydamas of Cyrene preferred to swallow his own teeth rather than spit them out and let his opponent know he'd knocked them out!

SLAVE

Terrible treatment

Whether they were captured by slave traders during wartime or sold into slavery by their own poverty-stricken families, life for the slaves of ancient Greece was not much fun. Being a slave was a common fate, too. Athens, for example, held around 250,000 people of which some 75,000-100,000 were slaves.

Treatment of slaves varied across the city states. In some, beatings and humiliation were considered acceptable, while in contrast one 5th-century visitor complained that in Athens, 'it is not permitted to strike slaves'. In general, slaves could not own property and did not have the same rights as free people. For example, slaves could be tortured as part of being questioned about a crime and, instead of being allowed to pay a fine for a minor crime, were often flogged.

Slaving away

The first few moments as a household slave could be pleasant, as slaves were often welcomed to their owner's home with fruits and nuts. It wouldn't be long, though, before they were set to work. They toiled for long hours in the home, cooking, cleaning and nursing children, or out in the fields, tending crops and livestock.

> Slaves carry food and dishes into a feast on tables balanced on their heads. Thousands of slaves worked in households. In the best cases, they were treated like a member of the family.

Many slaves worked in farms, orchards and olive groves. They climbed trees to pick olives which were then squeezed in an olive press to make olive oil.

WORK MATES

HELOTS: When Sparta conquered the neighbouring state of Messenia, all of Messenia's people effectively became slaves of Sparta. Known as Helots, most stayed living in their own homes but were forced to give up at least half of their crops to the Spartans. If that wasn't bad enough, every autumn, it was not a crime for a Spartan to beat or even murder a helot.

Some slaves were put to work at their owner's workplace. An Athenian man called Lysias, for instance, owned 120 slaves who all worked making soldiers' shields. Far worse was being put to work down narrow, one-metre-high tunnels in Greek silver mines. There, slaves faced the threat of death from exhaustion, rock falls or suffocation.

JOB VERDICT

Pretty grim, with few rights. All you can hope for is that one day you'll be granted (or able to buy) your freedom.

SOLDIER

Bring your own armour

Some Greek city-states employed foot soldiers called hoplites. These men needed to be tough and hardy. They had to march long distances over hilly ground on foot, often carrying their food, which included cheese, salted meats and onions, with them. Some made journeys by sea, as many Greek warships carried around 20 hoplites on their decks.

Hoplites would be armed with 2-2.5 m-long spears known as doru and often a short sword called a xiphos. Armour wasn't provided and bronze breastplates, helmets and greaves (a little like long metal shin pads) were expensive. Poorer hoplites had to make do with linen strips glued together and covered in animal skin or bronze scales.

JOB VACANCY
Start date: 500 BCE

- ARE YOU INTERESTED IN TRAVELLING THE KNOWN WORLD BY SEA AND LAND?
- DO YOU ENJOY FIGHTING? ARE YOU SKILLED AT HANDLING A SPEAR, SWORD AND SHIELD?
- ARE YOU BRAVE ENOUGH TO STARE DOWN A MIGHTY BAND OF ENEMY SOLDIERS?
- DOES YOUR FAMILY HAVE A SET OF BRONZE ARMOUR YOU COULD WEAR?

Hoplites were named after the hoplon – their round, heavy wooden shield covered in bronze. The 8- to 12-kg shields were not only for defence. They could prove a hefty weapon to batter the enemy to the ground.

A soldier at seven

If you were a boy in the city-state of Sparta, becoming a soldier wasn't an option, it was an order! Boys as young as seven were taken from their families to a military camp or school, known as the agoge, where they were trained in incredibly harsh conditions. Recruits weren't allowed underwear, sandals or even a bed, and were regularly underfed and beaten as it was thought that this treatment would toughen them up. Spartan men served in the army as part of their agoge until the age of 30 when, if they'd survived, they would be made a citizen of Sparta.

ODD JOB

YOU TREMBLER!

Spartan soldiers were renowned for their incredible fierceness, but some lost their nerve in training or battle and were called the most hurtful name in Spartan society — a 'trembler'! They would be mocked, shunned by friends and even forced to parade around Sparta with their hands tied in front of them like a prisoner.

Leonidas was the famed military leader of Sparta who died at the Battle of Thermopylae in 480 BCE. Like many ancient Greek soldiers he added a crest of horsehair to the top of his helmet to make himself look taller and more fearsome.

JOB VERDICT

A potentially solid career choice if you're brave, like the outdoor life and are part of a strong, dominant army. But if the force you join is weak and loses in battle, be prepared to become a slave as a result.

MARKET TRADER

A trader or seller's workplace was the agora, the open area in the centre of most ancient Greek settlements where markets were held. Traders and sellers would jostle for a good spot in the agora. There they might sell fish, cheeses or meat off a marble slab to keep the food cold, craftwork such as pottery, tools or jewellery, or spices, rugs and perfumes brought in by ship from abroad. The agora was the place to meet for ancient Greeks so it would be crowded and busy; traders needed a loud voice to make themselves heard above the noise of the market.

ODD JOB
MARKET VALUES

Market traders would sell to slaves and men first, as only a woman who was poor would come alone to the agora. There were no bags to carry shopping home in, and traders weren't surprised when soldiers used their helmets to transport olive oil or other liquids!

JOB VERDICT

Good, if you're canny at striking bargains for your goods and stay on the right side of the market officials.

MARKET OFFICIAL

According to Herodotus, an ancient Greek historian, Cyrus, the King of Persia called an agora, 'a special place marked out where Greeks meet to cheat each other'! To ensure fairness, many Greek city-states employed various officials at markets. Agoranomoi would check the quality of goods while metronomoi made sure that traders were selling fair amounts of their goods. A metronomoi was issued with a set of standard size containers and lead weights which he could use to check whether traders were being honest or short-changing their customers. Punishments varied from fines to removing the seller's goods and selling them at a public auction.

JOB VACANCY
Start date: 1500 BCE

- DO YOU HAVE A STRONG BELIEF IN RIGHT AND WRONG?
- ARE YOU GOOD AT NUMBERS, PRECISE AT WEIGHING THINGS AND A STICKLER FOR DETAIL?
- CAN YOU HANDLE ANGRY CUSTOMERS AND MARKET TRADERS WELL?

This container held an official measure of grain such as wheat or barley called a *choinike*, which was equal to 3.2 litres.

JOB VERDICT

A steady job, but one that would never make you rich nor win you popularity with all the sellers in the agora.

11

PLAYWRIGHT

Play for the day

Ancient Greece was the first known civilization to enjoy plays. These were performed at the foot of a sloping hill in an area called a theatron, meaning 'watching place'. Over time, dedicated theatre buildings were constructed, in which audiences paid to watch plays.

For much of the ancient Greek era, plays would be performed only by male actors. Most actors wore masks with exaggerated expressions, to communicate each character's mood to the audience. Some plays lasted all day, so playwrights needed plenty of stamina, as well as a long story and a supply of papyrus scrolls to write on. The plays were either comedies or tragedies – playwrights never mixed the two styles.

Euripedes wrote more than 90 plays, including the tragedies 'The Trojan Women' and 'Hippolytus'. He won the City Dionysia festival (see page 13) four times.

JOB VACANCY
Start date: 500 BCE

- ARE YOU KEEN ON LONG STORIES AND GOOD AT WRITING THEM?
- DO YOU COME FROM A WEALTHY FAMILY OR HAVE FRIENDS IN HIGH PLACES?
- CAN YOU DIRECT ACTORS AND HELP PUT ON A GRAND SHOW?

A collection of masks used in ancient Greek theatres. Some masks had a different facial expression on each side, so the actor could turn them round depending on his character's mood.

In competition

Playwrights made a living through payments from the state or a wealthy patron, or by winning competitions. In Athens, playwrights competed at the City Dionysia festival in honour of the Greek god, Dionysius, which lasted most of a week. Wealthy citizens of Athens paid for the plays to be put on as a form of tax and, along with the playwright, received a share of the prizes if they won.

If you and your plays were especially liked, you might find yourself being looked after by a powerful patron. The playwright Sophocles, for example, was made a treasurer of Athens and later a general by Pericles, the powerful ruler of Athens in the middle of the 5th century.

Actors in a scene from 'Medea' by Euripides, which is still performed today. Some plays included special effects, such as when a wooden crane called a mechane whisked an actor into the air to simulate flying.

ODD JOB

A FINE TRAGEDY

In 493 BCE, the playwright Phyrynichus produced a powerful tragedy, 'The Capture of Miletus', that made many of the audience weep with sadness. Poor old Phyrynichus was fined 1,000 drachmas as a result. That was equal to more than two years' pay for a farmer or metalworker!

JOB VERDICT

Promising. If your plays are enjoyed by the wealthy as well as by the masses, you can expect high status and plenty of funds to write your next one.

POLITICIAN

Votes for some, but not for all

The ancient Greek world was made up of a large number of individual city-states. Some of these, such as Megara, were ruled by a single king or tyrant for long periods, while others including Syracuse and Corinth, gave a far larger number of people a say in government. In Athens, it was proclaimed that everyone could vote on issues…well everyone except slaves, foreigners and women, who together made up more than two-thirds of the population. The remainder – the free men of Athens who could vote – were called citizens. Many of them would gather at the *ekklesia* or assembly where issues were debated and laws were passed.

JOB VACANCY
Start date: 500 BCE

- ARE YOU POPULAR AND GOOD AT MAKING FRIENDS AND FORMING ALLIANCES?
- DO YOU LIKE SPEAKING IN PUBLIC AND GETTING YOUR OWN WAY?
- CAN YOU MEMORIZE LONG, STIRRING SPEECHES AND DELIVER THEM WITH POWER AND CONVICTION?

ODD JOB

DASTARDLY DRACO

Draco was an Athenian politician who, in around 621 BCE, wrote down the first set of laws for his city-state. Draco went too far and his laws were incredibly harsh. They included selling people into slavery if they had debts, and giving them the death penalty for stealing a cabbage!

Athenian men gather together to debate a new law. By having powerful allies and followers at an assembly one politician could get his way over others.

Risks and rewards

Being a successful politician could bring big rewards, often in the form of being appointed to a public job such as being a magistrate or inspector of taxes, which was paid for by the state. But a career in politics in ancient Greece always carried risk with it. You might fall out of favour, suggest the wrong action or try to grab too much power, in which case you might become the subject of a public vote. If enough members of the assembly wrote your name down, you would be banished from the city-state. In Athens, Cimon had been a war hero after helping to defeat the Persians but was later banished for 10 years for a failed attempt to support the Spartans.

This piece of broken pottery, called an ostracon, was etched with the name of a politician during a vote for banishment. The pottery gave the process its name, to ostracize someone.

JOB VERDICT

An excellent job choice if you're a wealthy Greek man. You get the chance to influence how your city-state is run and help decide whether it makes war or alliances with other states.

ARCHITECT

Strictly perfect

Architects needed a brilliant eye for design and a thorough understanding of materials to create truly stunning temples and other public buildings. They would need a good knowledge of maths and geometry as well, as the ancient Greeks were firm believers in buildings being designed in strict proportions. For example, certain types of column had to be six or nine times as high as their diameter.

Big buildings were constructed out of stone, often marble, which cost much to quarry and transport to the building site. The stone had to be perfectly carved, as the Greeks did not use cement to stick each block together. Instead, the weight of the stone and, sometimes, metal clamps held it all together.

JOB VACANCY!
Start date: 500 BCE

- DO YOU HAVE A GOOD EYE FOR GEOMETRY AND DESIGN?

- ARE YOU SKILLED AT MANAGING LARGE NUMBERS OF WORKERS UNDER YOUR COMMAND?

- DO YOU KNOW THE DIFFERENCE BETWEEN YOUR IONIC AND YOUR DORIC COLUMNS?

The Parthenon was a temple designed by the architects Ictinus and Callicrates. It cost around 469 talents of silver at a time when as little as a single talent would buy an entire trireme, the most advanced warship of the age.

ODD JOB

COSTLY COLUMNS

The costs of an architect's vision could be eye-wateringly huge. A skilled workman earned one or two drachmas per day. A single elaborate column, such as these on the Temple of Athena in Athens, could cost as much as 40,000 drachmas!

Under pressure

For the best-known architects, life could be pretty good and you might count important politicians and generals as your friends. Wealthy city-states such as Corinth and Athens wanted nothing but the best buildings, and you would be paid handsomely to design them. But there was enormous pressure to get the construction right as the architect would oversee all the processes at every stage – from visiting the quarries to hiring the best stonemasons and ensuring that all parts of the project went well.

JOB VERDICT!

Very good for those who were successful. You'd be given major monuments to design with the chance that some of your work would still be standing 2,000 years later.

MERCHANT

Trading places

Trade was absolutely vital to city-states throughout the ancient Greek world. Many states could not grow enough of a variety of food to feed their people or needed the raw materials, from grapes to metals, with which to make other products. Merchants filled these gaps by buying cargoes of food, materials and other products from one place and transporting it to another where they hoped to sell at a large profit. They might buy timber from Cyprus, pottery from Corinth, grain and vegetables from Cyrene in North Africa or wool and meat from colonies on the Italian coast.

A merchant ship leaves the port of Delos with its cargo of fruit and cereal crops. Many merchant ships used large sails but some also had oarsmen on board (see panel).

WORK MATES

OARSMAN: A high pain threshold and great physical fitness were required to row with a giant wooden oar on board a merchant ship or trireme warship. The job could be gruelling, with the risk of drowning if the ship sank or injury if it was captured by pirates or an enemy navy. Many oarsmen were slaves who were forced to row the ship but amazingly, some were free men who chose to do it!

A risky business

Most merchants had just a single ship and not enough money to buy an entire cargo so they borrowed money from bankers or money lenders. The rate of interest could vary from 10 per cent to 100 per cent, even for a short trading trip lasting a few weeks.

To be a successful merchant, you would need to be excellent at both seafaring and business. You would need to target what a particular city-state needed the most and supply it with those goods before other merchants could do so ahead of you. Threats to your profitability ranged from choosing the wrong cargo to piracy and shipwreck, making it a very risky business for some.

Many cargoes – from grain to olive oil – were carried in large pottery amphorae.

JOB VERDICT

Being a merchant was a precarious existence, with storms, pirates or a poor choice of cargo threatening to ruin you, especially if you owed money to a banker. But with a bit of luck and by making the right choices, you could become rich.

PRIEST

* ARE YOU HEALTHY AND FREE OF DEBT?
* CAN YOU JUGGLE YOUR OTHER JOBS AND DUTIES TO DEVOTE TIME TO THE TEMPLE?
* WOULD YOU NOT BE SQUEAMISH ABOUT KILLING ANIMALS OR WORRIED ABOUT WEALTH?

Lots of gods

Religion was a very important part of every ancient Greek's life. The ancient Greeks worshipped a large number of gods and goddesses from Ares, the god of war, to Aphrodite, the goddess of love and beauty. The worship mostly took place at home, but there were many temples too, each dedicated to a particular god and staffed by priests.

Not everyone could be a priest. Army deserters, people in debt and those with a disability were not accepted. It was, however, one of the few public jobs available to a woman. Women became priestesses to a number of female gods, such as Hera, the goddess of weddings and marriage and Demeter, the goddess of agriculture.

This work, by a vase painter called Oltos, shows Zeus, the king of the gods (left) and Hestia (right), goddess of architecture and the hearth.

Dedicated to the Greek god of the sea, the Temple of Poseidon at Sounion sits overlooking the Aegean Sea and was completed around 440 BCE.

A priest's duties

Unlike some other civilizations, ancient Greek priests mainly worked part-time and were not expected to offer direct religious advice. They were mostly employed to look after the temple and to help make offerings to the gods. Priests would be present when the most common form of offering was made – by killing a farm animal such as a cow, goat or pig close to the temple. Frequently, part of the animal was left as an offering whilst the rest was cooked straight away, with the priest usually getting a share of the meat.

The Priestess of Dionysus.

WORK MATES

ORACLES: An oracle was a type of priestess who was thought to be able to speak directly to the gods. A number of temples had an oracle, but people throughout the entire ancient Greek world would make long journeys and pay, often in gold, to hear the most famous of all at the Temple of Apollo in Delphi. The Oracle of Delphi (below) only gave prophecies on the seventh day of each month and was never doubted.

JOB VERDICT

Low pay and only part-time work, but being a priest could often give you extra importance in your local community as well as free meat at sacrifice time.

SPORTSMAN

Great games

Games honouring the gods were held throughout the ancient Greek world. They included the Pythian Games at Delphi and from 776 BCE,

the Olympic Games at Olympia. For aspiring sportsmen (women were not allowed to compete), these Games gave them opportunities to compete in a range of sports. For the fleet of foot there were sprints over the length of a stade (around 180 to 190 m) in addition to longer races, as well as the long jump and discus and javelin throws. For those who liked a fight, there was boxing, wrestling and the *pankration* – a no-holds-barred, combat contest.

Competitors such as discus throwers took part in intense training at a *gymnasion* before a major Games. The athletes trained and competed naked, their skin rubbed with olive oil.

This scene painted on an ancient Greek vase shows Winged Victory crowning a winner at the Games at Olympia with a garland of woven olive leaves called a *kotinos*.

ODD JOB

OATHS AND RULES

Athletes at the ancient Games at Olympia had to swear an oath to compete fairly. They swore this in front of a terrifying 12m-high statue of Zeus with their hand on a slice of raw wild boar flesh. If runners at the ancient Olympics false-started, an official called a *mastigophoroi* or *alytai* would flog them with a whip!

Winners' rewards

Winners at the Games could expect large prizes – from horses to a giant amphora full of precious olive oil. Champions received further rewards on their return home. In the 6th century, the city of Athens granted winners at Olympia 500 drachma plus free meals for life! Winners in other city-states might be exempt from taxes or receive houses or slaves in tribute. The fame of a champion might prove a good base for a career in politics. Gelo won the chariot racing at Olympia in 488 BCE. Three years later, he became ruler of Syracuse.

Two competitors fight during a *pankration* bout. This sport could be brutal. One champion, Sostratos of Sicyon, was said to break his opponent's fingers one-by-one until they gave in!

JOB VERDICT

Competition is fierce, but if you survive the Games and are crowned champion, you could be set up for life.

PHILOSOPHER

Think about it

There was no one career path or training to become a philosopher in ancient Greece other than being incredibly curious about the world and coming up with original ideas to explain it. Socrates was the son of a stonemason and served as a hoplite in the Athenian army, while Pythagoras's father cut gemstones and Aristotle's dad was a doctor. Whether from rich backgrounds or poor, some philosophers were granted public jobs or became tutors to nobles or kings. Aristotle, for example, tutored a young boy who would go on to conquer the entire Greek world – Alexander the Great.

JOB VACANCY
Start date: 500 BCE

- ARE YOU A BIG THINKER? DO YOU LOVE TO WRESTLE WITH PROBLEMS IN YOUR HEAD?
- CAN YOU EXPLAIN YOUR THOUGHTS CLEARLY, ARGUE AND CONVINCE PEOPLE TO SEE YOUR POINT?
- ARE YOUR IDEAS REVOLUTIONARY AND CAPABLE OF CHANGING HOW PEOPLE THINK ABOUT THE WORLD?

The philosopher Socrates passed on his ideas through intense discussions with others, known as dialogues. For Socrates, 'a life without questions is no life at all'.

This Roman mosaic shows Plato (fourth left) at his school with others including Aristotle (right). Some philosophers set up their own schools where people could meet, learn and take part in discussions. Plato's Academy was founded in 378 BCE and continued for several centuries.

Thinking big, being brave

Philosophers spent most of their lives considering all sorts of issues, from how the Earth works to how people should live their lives. Some wrote their ideas down, fragments of which survive to this day. Others lived and died in poverty and anonymity. Part of the role of philosophers was to challenge the way in which people looked at things. This could bring them into conflict with either regular people who might mock them or political leaders or generals who might banish them or, in the case of Socrates, put them on trial.

When is a door not a door, Diogenes?

When it's a jar (sigh). Leave me alone!

Socrates was found guilty in 400 BCE of corrupting the minds of young men and was sentenced to death by drinking poisonous hemlock.

JOB VERDICT

Mixed. You might be celebrated as a great brain and showered with honours or shunned, banished and laughed at for your crazy ideas. Either way, you would carry on thinking.

25

CRAFTSMAN

Keep it in the family

Many ancient Greeks and metics (foreigners who settled in ancient Greece) were skilled at craftwork, capable of working with wood, leather, stone, metals or pottery. In smaller settlements, a single person or family might produce all the stone work or wood work required, but in larger towns and cities, craftworkers tended to specialise. Craftwork was often a family business. The son of a carpenter, potter or jewellery maker would serve as an apprentice to his own father for many years before either inheriting the family's workshop or striking out on his own.

JOB VACANCY
Start date: 500 BCE

● ARE YOU PATIENT AND HAPPY TO SIT IN THE SAME PLACE FOR HOURS ON END?

● ARE YOU HIGHLY SKILLED WITH YOUR HANDS AND QUITE ARTISTIC?

● DO YOU COME FROM A FAMILY OF CRAFT WORKERS?

NOTE: SLAVES AND METICS MAY APPLY!

It took years of experience before a craftsman could make an object as stunning as this gold krater – a two-handled container for mixing wine and water.

Pottering about

Despite some opportunities for showing artistic flair, especially in the creation of stone and bronze sculptures and fine gold objects, most craft work often meant long, repetitive days and repeated prayers to Hephaistos, the god of fire, volcanoes and craft workers. Craftsmen of a similar type might set up workshops in the same part of the town or city in order to share ideas and resources. Many potters in ancient Athens, for example, could be found in part of the city called Kerameikos. Potters worked clay all day, fashioning it into vases, jugs, cookware and amphora – large containers used to store olive oil, wine and other liquids.

This amphora shows a scene of a shoemaker cutting leather around the foot of a young boy. The shoemaker's tools are on a rack on the wall above his head.

This clay sculpture shows an ancient Greek carpenter sawing wood. Most craftsmen worked on their own for themselves, but some grew successful and employed others.

ODD JOB

SUPER-BUSY SCULPTOR

The sculptor Lysippos is estimated to have made more than 1,500 different sculptures during his lifetime in the 4th century, all fashioned out of bronze. His brother, Lysistratus was also a sculptor and possibly the first to use plaster to take impressions of faces of living people to help the accuracy of his work.

JOB VERDICT

Far from the worst. Other Greeks might look down on you for working with your hands, but you'd receive a similar rate of pay to a soldier and without the risk of injury and death in battle.

DOCTOR

Gods and doctors

Early Greek doctors were mostly priests who worked in temples dedicated to Asclepius, the god of healing. Their job was straightforward – to wait with an ill person who had come to a temple hoping to be healed. During the ancient Greek era, advances were made in medicine, and some doctors understood that diseases were natural and not caused by gods. Hippocrates worked as a doctor on the island of Kos and was a major pioneer of a more scientific approach, believing that a patient needed to be questioned and observed closely to make a diagnosis.

JOB VACANCY
Start date: 500 BCE

- DO YOU HAVE A PASSION FOR HEALING PEOPLE AND TRYING TO EASE SUFFERING?
- HAVE YOU MEMORIZED DOZENS OF DIFFERENT REMEDIES INVOLVING PLANTS, HERBS AND OTHER INGREDIENTS?
- ARE YOU CONFIDENT ENOUGH TO CONVINCE PEOPLE YOU KNOW WHAT YOU ARE DOING?
- CAN YOU AVOID FAINTING AT THE SIGHT OF BLOOD?

Patients at the temple of Asclepius often left behind a model of the ill part of their body as an offering to the god, like this clay model of a stomach.

Hippocrates was one of the first doctors to use words such as chronic and epidemic to describe diseases. He devised the Hippocratic Oath which new doctors would take, vowing to keep a patient's condition secret and not to poison patients.

Medical skills

Operations would have been agony for patients, as doctors had no anaesthetics and worked with unsterilized bronze knives and other tools.

As a doctor in the later Greek era, you could set yourself up in practice with next-to-no-training. All you'd need were patients who believed in your healing abilities. Or you could choose to work under a more senior doctor for a few years to build your experience. Your remedies would include potions made of many natural ingredients, bloodletting (making a cut to release blood from the body) and on some occasions, surgery. If you were successful, there were great rewards to be had. Demoekedes of Kroton was one renowned doctor who was paid roughly 40 times the rate of a skilled worker to be resident doctor at Samos.

ODD JOB

GROSS GREEK

Hippocrates devised a remedy to cure baldness — a lotion containing beetroot, horseradish, nettles and pigeon droppings! He would also taste a patient's ear wax and even their wee to try to diagnose what was wrong.

JOB VERDICT

Very good if you gained a reputation for being a gifted healer.

QUIZ

Which job in ancient Greece would you be most suited to? Answer the questions below then turn the book upside down to read the verdict!

Questions

1 **Do you want to explore and travel the world?**

a) You betcha!

b) I don't mind some travelling.

c) I'd rather stay at home and do something safe instead.

2 **Are you competitive, like taking risks and able to convince others to do so too?**

a) Yes, I live for the thrill of risk and a challenge.

b) I am good at talking to others but not very competitive.

c) Nope, not for me. I'm not a risk taker at all.

3 **Are you patient and good with your hands?**

a) No, not very although I can tie knots.

b) I have some patience and can do some things with my hands.

c) Yes, I am good with fiddly things and have bags of patience.

4 **Are you good at reading, numbers and remembering things?**

a) I'm good with numbers and maps.

b) Yes, I have a very good memory and I enjoy reading and thinking.

c) Not particularly, I prefer to do practical things.

Answers

Mostly As
You may be cut out to be an ancient Greek merchant or trader, or even a politician.

Mostly Bs
It appears you might be suited to being a doctor or even a philosopher in ancient Greece.

Mostly Cs
Sounds like you might make an excellent ancient Greek craftsman.

Glossary

agora The central meeting place in most ancient Greek cities.

chronic Describes an illness that lasts for a long time or keeps coming back.

city-state An independent state in ancient Greece made up of a city and the land it controlled.

colony An overseas settlement.

diagnosis An identification by a doctor of what is wrong with a patient after examining the patient's symptoms.

epidemic Describes a disease that spreads widely through a community.

hoplite An ancient Greek foot soldier.

jury The people in a law court who listen to evidence and decide whether someone is guilty or innocent.

oracle A type of priestess who was thought by the ancient Greeks to be able to speak directly to the gods.

ostracon A piece of broken pottery on which a vote for banishment was written.

pankration A type of violent wrestling that took place at the ancient Greek Games, with almost no rules.

suffocation To die due to a lack of air or oxygen in air to breathe.

trireme A Greek warship with three banks or rows of oars.

tyrant An absolute ruler of an ancient Greek territory or city-state.

Zeus The king of the ancient Greek gods and the most powerful of the gods.

Further Information

Books

The History Detective Investigates: Ancient Greece – Rachel Minay (Wayland, 2014)

Food and Cooking in Ancient Greece – Clive Gifford (Wayland, 2014)

At Home With The Ancient Greeks – Tim Cooke (Wayland, 2014)

Hail! Ancient Greeks – Jen Green (Wayland, 2013)

History from Objects: The Greeks – John Malam (Wayland, 2012)

Websites

http://www.childrensuniversity.manchester.ac.uk/interactives/history/greece/
Check out the interactive map of ancient Greece and learn about events in this website's timeline.

http://www.ancientgreece.co.uk/
Learn more about the ancient Greek gods, festivals, daily life and wars at this British Museum website.

http://www.penn.museum/sites/olympics/olympicorigins.shtml
Lots more facts on the ancient Games at Olympia and who took part in them.

http://carlos.emory.edu/ODYSSEY/GREECE/home.html
A fun, animated visual guide to life in ancient Greece, including information on daily life, ancient Greek gods, city-states and architecture.

INDEX